October 2019

To Brynn, Owen and Emmy

May God always bless you
with joy, health, laughter & love.

Grandma & Papa Lingaur
xoxo

Given to

....

on the occasion of

....

on

....

Candle
PRAYERS
for Kids

By Claire Freedman
Illustrated by Jo Parry

CANDLE
BOOKS

Published by Candle Books
an imprint of
Lion Hudson plc
Wilkinson House, Jordan Hill Road,
Oxford OX2 8DR, England
www.lionhudson.com/candle

ISBN 978 1 78128 102 4
e-ISBN 978 1 78128 146 8

First edition 2014

Acknowledgments
The Lord's Prayer (on page 128) is adapted from the Contemporary English Version.
Copyright © 1991, 1992, 1995 by American Bible Society.

A catalogue record for this book is available from the British Library

Printed and bound in China, April 2014, LH23

Contents

LET'S PRAISE GOD!

Dear God, we praise you.
Dear Lord, we love you.
What would we do without you?
Thank you, God.
Amen.

Clap your hands and shout for joy,
God loves every girl and boy.
Praise God!

God is good, God is kind, God is great,
Let's thank him!

Dear God,
I like praising you,
I like singing to you at the top of my voice!
Thank you for praise time, God.
Amen.

Hooray! God made the
giraffe as tall as a tree.
Let's praise him.
Hooray! God made the
caterpillar, ant, and bee.
Let's thank him.
Hooray! God made our world,
so perfectly.
Hooray for God!

Let all the little children praise their Lord,
For he loves them, one and all!
Praise God!

OUR FAMILIES AND FRIENDS

Dear God,
Thank you for happy, loving feelings.
Thank you for cuddles with Mummy and Daddy.
Thank you for hugs and kisses.
Dear God, thank you for giving me so much love.
Amen.

Dear God,
I love my mummy and daddy.
I love my brother and sister.
I love my gran and grandpa.
Please look after us all.
Please don't forget to look after me, too, Lord.
Thank you,
Amen.

Dear God,
Thank you for my family.
Thank you for all the people who look after me.
Please look after all the children who don't have
    families of their own.
Thank you, God.
Amen.

Dear God,
My best friend has moved to another city.
She lives so far away from me now, God.
I really miss her.
Please help us both to make new best friends
    very soon.
Then we won't feel so sad.
Thank you, God. Amen.

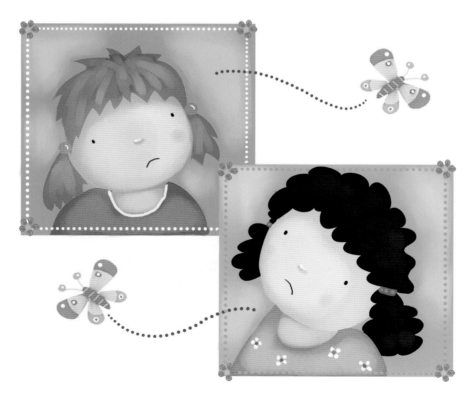

Dear God,
My uncle and auntie came to visit.
They brought me a huge teddy.
My uncle told me funny jokes.
Thank you for my uncle and auntie, God.
Goodnight, God.
P.S. Teddy says goodnight, too!

Dear God,
My daddy has to go away for his work.
He will be gone for a whole week.
Please look after Daddy while he is away.
Please help his work to go well.
And, please God, bring Daddy home safely to
   Mummy and me.
Thank you,
Amen.

Dear God,
My friend broke my toy today.
I know he didn't mean to, Lord,
   but it was my best toy.
Please help me to forgive my friend.
Amen.

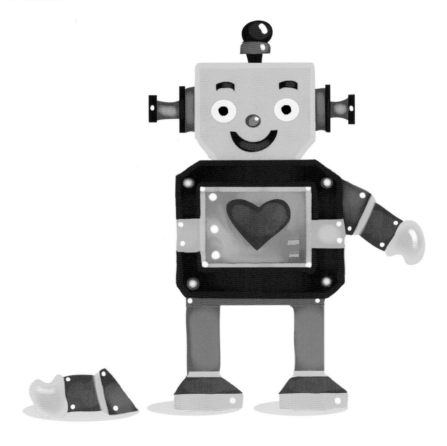

Dear God,
Great news!
My brand new baby sister is here at last.
She looks very small, God.
Her fingers are tiny.
I can't wait to play with her.
Please help her grow up really fast, so I can.

Dear God,
Sometimes I find my brother very annoying.
I get fed up with him.
Please help me to get on better with my brother.
Please help me to feel more loving towards him.
Thank you,
Amen.

Dear God,
Daddy has to work so hard.
We hardly ever see him.
Please help Daddy at work,
    so he can come home earlier.
Then I can kiss him goodnight
    before I go to sleep.
Thank you, God.
Amen.

Dear God,
Thank you for friends to play with.
Thank you that we can play games
   and have fun together.
Thank you, God.
Amen.

Dear God,
Please forgive me.
Today I was unkind to my friend.
Please help us to make up tomorrow.
Amen.

GRACES

It's dinner time!
Help us to remember that it is you, dear God,
  who gives us our food each day.
Thank you, Lord.
And please help us to remember our
  table manners!

For our drink,
For our food.
For your gifts that are so good.
We thank you, God.

SPECIAL DAYS

Dear God,
I had the best birthday party ever.
All my friends came.
They gave me lots of cards and presents.
I blew all the candles out on my cake in one puff.
Thank you for a wonderful birthday, God.
Amen.
P.S. Thank you for my mummy.
She worked hard to make my day happy.

SCHOOL

Dear God,
I didn't have a very nice time at school today.
I got all my sums wrong.
Please help me to try harder at my lessons.
Thank you,
Amen.

Dear God,
Thank you for our school.
Our teacher is really kind and helpful.
She's so good at explaining things to me.
She makes work easier to understand.
Thank you for my teacher and my school,
   Lord.
Our lessons are a lot of fun.
I really enjoy learning things.

Dear God,
I am starting my new school tomorrow.
I am really scared, God.
There are big butterflies in my tummy.
Please come to school with me,
    and help me make new friends.
Thank you, God.
Amen.

Dear God,
Please help me with my work at school.
Sometimes I find it hard.
Please help me to listen to my teacher
  more carefully.
Please help me not to give up too quickly
  when I find work difficult.
Thank you, God. Amen.

Dear God,
Sometimes I'm scared of people at school.
I'm scared of standing up in class.
I don't like it when everyone looks at me.
I'm worried I'll get all my words muddled up.
Everyone will laugh at me, God.
They will think I am stupid.
Please be with me, dear God.
Please help me in school.
Thank you.
Amen.

HOLIDAY TIME! HAPPY TIME!

Dear God,
Thank you for school holidays.
Help us to use the time well and not waste it.
Thank you,
Amen.

Today we fed the ducks, Lord.
Mum saved up all the bread.
They waddled out to say "hello",
All waiting to be fed.

We counted lots of ducklings,
And heard them "quack, quack, quack",
I'm glad that you made ducks, Lord.
Please can we soon go back?

Dear God,
We're off on our holidays tomorrow.
I'm so excited.
Dear God, I'm glad that however
 far from home we are,
 you are always with us.
Even if we flew to the moon.

Dear God,
Thank you for all the fun of the seaside.
Thank you for sandcastles and sandy beaches.
Thank you for splashing in the waves and
   paddling in the sea.
Thank you for shells and seaweed,
   and rock pools to explore.
Thank you for picnics and ice creams
   on the beach.
Thank you for holidays, God. Amen.

Dear Lord,
I'm glad that, when we are
   far from home,
You are still with us.
Please keep us safe.
Amen

YOU KNOW HOW I FEEL...

Dear God,
I'm sorry I was so naughty today.
Please forgive me.
Sometimes I find it hard to be good.
Please help me to be nicer tomorrow.
Thank you, Lord.
Amen.

Dear God,
Please help me to tell the truth.
Even if I know it might get me into
    trouble with Mum.
Thank you, Lord.
Amen.

Sometimes I get all cross inside,
And have a bad mood day.
I scream and shout and stamp my feet,
If I don't get my way.

I'm sorry for my bad mood, God,
I just wanted to say,
I'm glad that when I'm good or bad,
You love me anyway.

Dear God,
I did something wrong today.
You know what it was, God.
I'm sorry.
Please forgive me.
Thank you, God.
Amen.

Dear God,
Today I told a fib.
I know it was wrong.
I haven't felt right inside ever since.
I'm sorry, God.
I won't do it again.
Thank you, God.
I feel better now.

Dear God,
I am SO disappointed.
I wanted to be the princess in our class play.
All I am going to be is a tree.
My friend is the princess.
Please help me to be pleased for her.
Please help me to be the best tree ever.
Thank you,
Amen.

Dear God,
Please help me to stop wanting things I know
    Mummy can't afford.
Like the latest PlayStation.
Or expensive toys.
Please help me to be grateful for all the
    things I do have.
Thank you, God.
Amen.

GOD AND ME

Dear God,
Knowing that you love me makes me feel
   all warm and happy inside.
Thank you, God.
Amen.

Dear God,
I'm glad you love me
I'm glad you are looking after me.
I feel a lot safer knowing that, Lord.
Thank you for everything.
Amen.

Dear God,
Please be close to me, today,
    tomorrow and always.
Amen.

Dear God,
Thank you, that with you
    I am never alone.
Amen.

Dear God,
You know all about me.
You know how many freckles I have on my face.
You know what I like to eat.
You know when I am happy or sad.
And you know what is best for me.
Thank you, God.
Amen.

Dear God,
Thank you that when we are sorry
   we can ask you for forgiveness.
Thank you that you always forgive us.
Amen.

Dear God,
I'm happy that even if I forget about you,
You will never forget about me.
Thank you, God.
Amen.

Dear God,
Thank you for prayer time.
Thank you that we can talk to you.
Anytime.
Anywhere.
Thank you that we can tell you
   the secrets of our hearts.
Our joys.
Our troubles.
Our hopes.
Our fears.
We can share them all with you.
Thank you, God. Amen.

Dear God,
Thank you!
You answered my prayer!
Everything went all right today.
You really helped me, God.
I won't feel so frightened next time.
Amen.

Dear God,
Sometimes I don't talk to you
   – but I know you're still there.
Thank you.
Amen.

THANK YOU, GOD

Dear God,
I saw a beautiful rainbow this afternoon.
It made me remember your story in the Bible
   about Noah and the flood.
Thank you, God.
Amen.

Dear God,
Thank you for television.
I like the animal shows best.
But please help me not to watch too much TV.
Thank you, God.
Amen.

Dear God,
Thank you for books to read.
Thank you that we can learn things from them
 and really enjoy reading.
Amen.

Dear God,
Thank you for music.
I like hearing happy songs on the radio.
I like listening to pop bands on TV.
Thank you for choirs and concerts and musicals.
I'm glad you made music, Lord.
Amen.

Dear God,
Thank you for my playgroup.
I like dressing up, painting,
    playing in the sandpit, and making things.
Oh, I also like story time too.
Thank you for playgroup, God.
Amen.

Dear God,
I love my bath time.
I have lots and lots of bubbles.
I pretend I'm swimming in the sea.
It's fun!
Thank you for my bath time, God.

Dear God,
Today my sister and I put on a play
   for Mummy and Daddy.
We dressed up in costumes.
Mummy and Daddy clapped at the end.
They said we were brilliant.
Thank you for today, God.
It was fun.
Please can I be an actor when I grow up?
Amen.

Dear God,
Please, please, please can our team
    win the match tomorrow?
Thank you, God.
Amen.

OUR PETS

My cat had kittens last night, God.
They are so tiny!
Please help them grow up big and strong.
Please find them all nice homes where
   they will be loved.
Thank you, God.
P.S. I promise I will play with them gently.

Dear God,
Thank you for my new puppy.
He is very naughty.
Please help me to look after him properly.
I want him to be happy living with us.
Amen.

PRAYERS FOR OTHERS

Dear God,
My mummy works very hard to look after me.
She doesn't have much time to look after herself.
Please will you look after her, God?
I promise to help.
Thank you.
Amen.

Dear God,
Where would we be without farmers?
They work hard in the fields all day,
  growing crops for our food.
Thank you for cows that give us milk.
And hens that lay us eggs.
Thank you for all the farm animals, God.
Amen.

Dear God,
I feel sad for all the children who don't know you.
They don't know what they are missing.
Thank you for being my God.
Please help other children to learn about you, too.
Amen.

Thank you for our daily food.
Our tummies are always full.
Please help all the poor children we see on TV
    who don't have enough to eat everyday.
They look so thin.

Dear God,
Thank you for the spider on my bedroom ceiling.
I don't know why some people are scared of
  spiders, God.
Especially Mummy.
Please help my mummy not to be
  so scared of spiders.

Dear God,
Thank you so much for my family.
I know that some children don't have a
    mummy or daddy to look after them.
They must feel very unhappy and scared.
Please look after all the lonely children
    everywhere, Lord.
Please find them new families of their own.
Thank you, Lord.
Amen.

Dear God,
Thank you that I have a comfortable home.
Not everyone does.
Please look after all the children
    who don't have a home of their own.
Thank you that I have friends and family around me.
Not everyone does.
Please look after all the lonely children.
Thank you that I have toys and books and games.
Not everyone does.
Please look after all the
    children who have
    nothing to play with.
Thank you for all the
    good things you
    give me, God.
Amen.

Dear God,
Thank you for the fishermen
    who go out in their boats everyday
    to catch us fish to eat.
Please look after them while they are at sea.
Thank you, God.
Amen.

Dear Father up in heaven,
Please help people in poor countries
    who don't have enough to eat.
Please send the rain so their crops will grow.
Please find people to help them.
Don't let them be forgotten, Lord.
Amen.

SAD TIMES

Dear God,
Sometimes Mummy and Daddy shout at each other.
I don't like it.
It makes me feel all wobbly inside.
Please help Mummy and Daddy not to argue.
Then we can all be happy.
I'm glad I can tell you about this, Lord.
Thank you,
Amen.

Dear God,
When I'm sad, please help me to be happy again.
Thank you for being with me.
Thank you for understanding how I feel.
Amen.

Dear God,
I miss my daddy.
I wish he still lived with us.
Dear God, please look after my daddy
   in his new home.
I'm glad I've got a Father in heaven
   – that's you.
Thank you, God.
Amen.

GOODNIGHT, GOD!

Dear God,
I like it when I lie in bed at night
   and listen to the wind and rain.
I feel so cosy and safe.
Thank you for my snuggly warm bed, Lord.
Please look after all the wild animals and
   birds outside in the cold.
Please find them somewhere safe and warm
   to shelter.
Thank you, Lord,
Amen.

As night-time comes creeping,
And children are sleeping,
God watches us, deep through the night.
So hush now, no peeping,
For God will be keeping,
You safe, till the new morning's light.
Amen.

Calm us, Lord, at the end of the day.
And hear our prayers as we come to pray.
Amen.

Bedtime blessings fall upon you,
All through the night.
May God's angels watch you sleeping,
Till the morning light.

Dear God,
Please look after me at bedtime.
Sometimes I wake up in the middle
 of the night and feel scared.
Help me to remember
 that you are always with me.
Then I won't need to be afraid.
Day and night, God, I'm glad you're
 my friend.

Soft moonbeams light the garden,
The sky is starry bright,
Dear Father up in heaven,
Please bless us all tonight.

Bless us in the morning,
Bless us through the day,
Bless us as we go to sleep,
And keep us safe, we pray.

May God bless you and keep you.
May he smile down upon you
And give you peace.

I'M SCARED, GOD

Dear God,
Sometimes I get lonely.
I am too shy to talk to anyone.
I feel very left out.
Please help me to fit in and make friends.
I know I always have a friend in you.
Thank you,
Amen.

Dear God,
I got lost in the shopping mall today.
I was very upset.
Mummy got upset too.
I promise never to run off on my own again.
I'm sorry.
Thank you for keeping me safe, Lord.
I'm glad you were looking after me
    when I was lost.
Amen.

Dear God,
We had a big storm today.
There was thunder and lightning,
  crashing and banging!
I felt frightened.
It was so loud I wanted to run away and hide.
Please help me not to be so afraid, God.
I know I don't need to be.
I know that you are looking after me.
Thank you, God.
Amen.

Dear God,
Please help me to be brave and strong, Lord.
I'm scared of so many things.
I'm scared of the big boys in the playground.
I'm scared of our friends' dog.
It always barks at me.
Please take away all my fears.
Thank you, God.
Amen.

Dear God,
Tomorrow is a very important day for me.
You know about it already.
Please look after me tomorrow.
Thank you for listening, God.
I'm not so worried now.

PRAYERS TO JESUS

Dear Lord Jesus,
You are a friend to all the little children.
Please be with all unhappy children, everywhere.
Thank you, Jesus.
Amen.

Dear Jesus,
Thank you for giving us the Bible,
  so we can learn more about you.
Amen.

Dear Lord Jesus,
Thank you that I can talk to you.
Thank you that I can tell you all my worries.
Thank you that you listen to my prayers.
Thank you that you help me.
Amen.

Dear Lord Jesus,
Please help me when I pray to you.
Please help me to know that you are there.
I want to grow closer to you, dear Lord.
Amen.

Dear Jesus,
I got into trouble today.
It wasn't my fault.
It's not fair, Lord.
I know that you weren't always treated fairly.
So you know how I feel.

Dear Jesus,
Thank you for loving me.
I love you too.
Amen.

Dear Lord Jesus,
You are full of love.
You are kind and caring.
Please help me to grow up just like you.
Amen.

Dear Lord Jesus,
You taught us to love our enemies.
It's not easy, Lord.
Please help me though.
Amen.

Dear Lord Jesus,
When I think of you
    I feel warm and safe inside.
Thank you,
Amen.

GOD'S AMAZING WORLD

Dear God,
Our world is millions of years old.
Yet we are still discovering some of the
    amazing things you made.
Like strange fish that live deep under the ocean.
And tiny creatures you need a big microscope
    to see.
God, you have always known they were there.
I think that's wonderful, God.

Dear God,
Today we went to the zoo.
I saw lots of animals you made.
Huge elephants, tiny lizards,
    chattering monkeys, gentle deer,
    waddling penguins, and prowling lions.
You made them all, God.
Big and small.
Thank you, God.
Amen.

Dear God,
Thank you for the changing seasons.
For the beauty of spring,
When lambs are born and flowers
   bloom everywhere.
For long hot summer days,
When we can play outside and
   enjoy the sunshine.
For autumn, when the fruit is
   ripe for picking,
And leaves tumble from
   the trees: red, gold,
   and yellow.
Thank you for the snows
   and ice of winter,
That turn our fields
   into white winter
   wonderlands.
Thank you for the
   seasons, God.
Amen.

Dear God,
A bird is building its nest in our garden.
Please keep the eggs safe, Lord.
Please look after the baby birds as they
    grow up and fly the nest.
Thank you, God.
Amen.

Dear God,
Thank you for trees.
Birds make their nests in the branches.
Squirrels and mice make their homes
   in the trunks and roots.

Thank you for tree blossom in spring.
Thank you for big shady trees
   to sit under in summer.
Thank you for autumn leaves
   to swish through.

Thank you for fruit trees:
   apple, plum, and pear,
   cherry, orange, and lemon.
Thank you for the trees.

Dear God,
Thank you for all things that grow.
Little acorns that grow into huge oak trees.
Small grains of corn that grow into fields
    of yellow wheat.
Thank you for all the tiny seeds that grow
    into flowers, fruit, and vegetables.
It's wonderful, Lord.
Amen.

Dear God,
Thank you for making the moon and stars.
Thank you for making comets, asteroids,
   and black holes.
The universe is so big and amazing, God.
You must have helped men to build rockets
   to fly into space.
Please God, one day can I go up in one?

HEALTH

Dear God,
I don't feel very well today.
Please make me better tomorrow.
Thank you for being with me, God.
Amen.

Dear God,
My grandad is in hospital.
He needs an operation.
Please make the operation go well, God.
Please help my grandad to get better quickly.
Please look after my granny too,
    and help her not to worry.
Thank you,
Amen.

Dear God,
My grandad is much better.
He's back home from hospital.
Thank you for all the doctors and nurses
    who looked after my grandad.
Thank you for answering my prayers, God.
Amen.

Dear God,
My friend didn't come to school today.
She isn't very well.
Please help my friend to get better soon.
Be with my friend and all sick children, Lord.
They need you.

Dear God,
Thank you for our health and strength.
Thank you that we can run and jump and skip.
Please look after all the children in wheelchairs
 who can't just get up and walk.
Amen.

Dear God,
I fell over in the playground.
Thank you for the school nurse
who made my sore knee better.
She made me smile again.

GOOD MORNING, GOD!

Dear God,
Thank you for this bright new morning.
Outside the sun is shining.
Birds are singing happily.
Everything looks fresh after the rain.
It makes me feel glad to be alive today, Lord.
Thank you, for such a beautiful day.

Good morning God!
Thank you for another day.
Please be with me as I go to school.
Please be with Daddy as he drives to work.
Please be with Mummy as she does her job.
Please let us all have a nice day.
Thank you,
Amen.

Dear God,
Last night I promised to be good today.
Please help me to keep my promise.
Thank you,
Amen.

Dear God,
I'm so glad you are here, when I wake up.
I'm glad I can ask you to look after me today.
It's good to know that you are taking care
   of everything.
Now I can start the day feeling really happy!
Hurrah!

DAY BY DAY

Dear God,
Thank you for all the delicious food you give us.
Thank you for jellies and ice cream,
    pizza and chips,
    cakes, sweets, and biscuits.
I love them all!
Thank you, Lord.
Amen.

Dear God,
We had a lovely time playing in the park, today.
Thank you.
Amen.

Dear God,
Thank you for my babysitter,
    who's looking after me tonight.
Please can Mummy and Daddy have a lovely time
    while they are out?
Please help me to sleep well.
Thank you, God.
Amen.

Dear God,
I accidentally kicked my football into next
  door's garden.
AGAIN.
Please help me to remember to be more
  careful next time.
Thank you that the people next door are kind
  and always throw my ball back.
Amen.

Dear God,
Sometimes I find it hard to share my toys
   with my friends.
I know it's wrong.
Please help me to share.
Thank you, God.
Amen.

Dear God,
I like it when it rains.
I love splashing in puddles.
Thank you for rain, God.
Amen.

Dear God,
You made us a beautiful world.
Help us not to drop litter and spoil it.
Thank you.
Amen.

Dear God,
I'm really excited!
I scored a goal in football.
It felt wonderful.
Thank you for games and sports
 and all the fun you give us.

Hello God,
Daddy and I sent a message to my cousin
   in Australia.
We sent it by email on the computer.
My cousin sent me a message straight back!
Thank you for making people so clever
   that they invented computers.

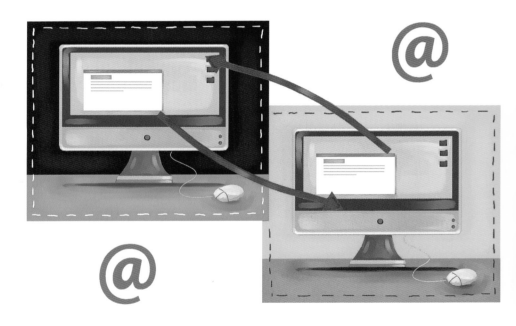

Dear God,
Today Mum bought me a beautiful sparkly
  pink ballerina dress.
It is just what I wanted, God.
I never, ever want to take my new dress off.
Thank you for my beautiful ballet dress.

Dear God,
All over the world, people pray to you in
    different languages.
You understand each and every one of us.
You listen to all our prayers.
Thank you, Lord.
Amen.

Dear God,
We have so much to say "thank you" for.
Our mummies and daddies, who love us,
Brothers and sisters and friends to play with.
Pets to cuddle and stroke.
Toys and games.
Parks and playgrounds.
Trees to climb.
Kites to fly.
And that's just the start, Lord.
Thank you for everything.
Amen.

Dear God,
Thank you for our church.
Thank you that we can go to church
   and sing songs to you.
I hope you enjoy listening to us, Lord.
Amen.

Hello God,
Nothing special happened today.
So I haven't anything very special to say.
Except that I'm glad that, to you,
I'm special in every way!

JESUS' PRAYER

Our Father in heaven,
help us to honour your name.
Come and set up your kingdom soon,
so that everyone on earth
will obey you,
as you are obeyed in heaven.
Give us our food for today.
Forgive us the wrong things we have done,
as we forgive other people.
Keep us from being tempted
and protect us from evil.
Amen.